OCTOPUSES!

STRANGE AND WONDERFUL

Laurence Pringle   Illustrated by Meryl Henderson

BOYDS MILLS PRESS

AN IMPRINT OF HIGHLIGHTS

Honesdale, Pennsylvania

Octopus hugs for Heidi, Jeffrey, Sean, Jesse, and Rebecca, with fond memories of all of our roughhousing games.
—LP

To Janice and Joe Lukas—my good friends.
—MH

Information sources for this book include the listed books, periodicals, and websites, but especially the following book written by three cephalopod researchers: Jennifer Mather, Roland Anderson, and James Wood. *Octopus: The Ocean's Intelligent Invertebrate*. Portland, OR: Timber Press, 2010.

The author thanks Dr. Jennifer Mather, Department of Psychology and Neuroscience, University of Lethbridge, Alberta, Canada, for her careful review of the text and illustrations.

Text copyright © 2015 by Laurence Pringle
Illustrations copyright © 2015 by Meryl Henderson

Boyds Mills Press
An Imprint of Highlights
815 Church Street
Honesdale, Pennsylvania 18431
boydsmillspress.com
Printed in China

ISBN: 978-1-59078-928-5
Library of Congress Control Number: 2014943964

First edition
10 9 8 7 6 5 4 3 2 1

The text is set in Goudy Old Style.
The illustrations are done in watercolor.

The shark was hungry. As it swam, its eyes scanned the water below, searching for food.

There! A brownish octopus was moving along the sandy bottom. The shark dived toward its prey. It lunged closer, closer. Its mouth gaped wide to grab the octopus.

Suddenly, the shark found itself in a dark underwater cloud. It couldn't see!

Its jaws snapped shut—on a mouthful of inky water.

The octopus, now pale white, jetted safely away.

Octopodes, not octopi!
Many people believe that another way to say "octopuses" is "octopi."
Some dictionaries say so. That would be true if this animal's name came from Latin. However, it comes from the ancient Greek word "octopous."
In Greek, the plural is "octopodes."

4

Within seconds, the octopus had released a cloud of ink, changed its body color, and jetted through the water. These are just some of the amazing abilities of octopuses that help them escape enemies.

Octopuses can also change their body shapes and even the texture of their skin. They can squeeze through tiny holes and crevices. Curious and smart, they can solve problems, learn quickly, and remember. Octopuses are the most intelligent of all **invertebrate** animals (those without backbones). They are probably smarter than many animals that have backbones, including reptiles and fish. Some scientists think that octopuses may be as smart as cats or dogs.

These brainy creatures are part of a huge animal group—the **mollusks**. There are more than 100,000 species (kinds) of mollusks. They all have soft bodies with no bones.

Most are protected by a hard outer shell. Mollusks include snails, clams, oysters, scallops, mussels, limpets, conchs, and cowries—the list can go on and on.

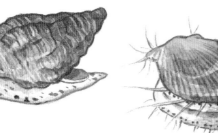

Clams and most other mollusks have a simple nervous system. In contrast, octopuses have a well-developed nervous system, a big brain, and keen eyes. They are part of a remarkable mollusk group called **cephalopods** (CEF-a-lo-pods). Cephalopod means "head-foots," with their limbs next to their heads. Cephalopods live only in salt water, and in every ocean. They include octopuses, squids, cuttlefish, and nautiluses.

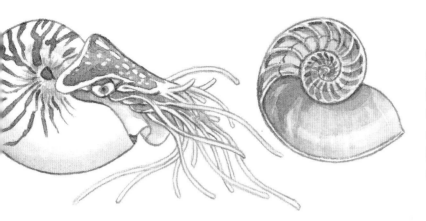

Nautiluses are the only cephalopods with an outer shell. The weight and shape of the shell makes them slow swimmers. They lack arms but have about ninety **tentacles**. (Tentacles are longer and thinner than arms.) Nautiluses have thirty or more walled spaces, or chambers, inside their shells. A nautilus can change the amount of water and gas (mostly nitrogen) in the chambers, which allows it to move up or down rather quickly.

Cuttlefish are not fish but cephalopods. The biggest of 120 cuttlefish species is only about three feet long. Cuttlefish catch small fish and other prey with suckers on their eight arms and on the tips of their two tentacles. Within their bodies is cuttlebone—a shell-like material riddled with small spaces. Like a nautilus, a cuttlefish can control the amounts of gas or water stored within those spaces to help it move up or down in the water.

Squids are the fastest-moving of all cephalopods. They are sometimes called "sprinters of the sea." Their bodies get some support from a long, thin inner piece of **cartilage**, called a pen. Like cuttlefish, squids have eight arms and two long, thin tentacles. Most of the nearly 300 squid species are less than a foot long. However, a squid is Earth's biggest cephalopod: the giant squid. Measured from one end of its body to the tips of its outstretched tentacles, it can grow to be sixty feet long (about as long as two big school buses). It also has the biggest eyes of any animal on Earth—the size of volleyballs or dinner plates.

7

Octopus species number about three hundred, including little-known kinds that drift freely in oceans or live deep underwater. They all have surprisingly short lives; most species live less than a year. The giant Pacific octopus may live up to three or four years. Whether an octopus is big or little, all species have the same key body parts, shown here.

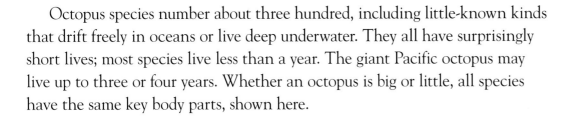

Mantle

The mantle may look like a head, but an octopus's head— with eyes, mouth, and brain—is connected to the baglike mantle. Within the muscular mantle are a stomach, kidneys, gills, other organs, and three hearts. Two of the hearts pump blood through the gills, where oxygen is taken from water. The other heart pumps blood carrying oxygen through the body and arms.

Funnel (Siphon)

The funnel, or siphon, carries water out of the mantle. Water is drawn in through slits in the mantle. After **gills** take vital oxygen from it, the water is pushed out the funnel. (Gills take oxygen from water; your lungs take oxygen from air.)

Arm

An octopus has eight powerful arms, and no tentacles. Each arm is lined with suckers. An octopus can control each arm and sucker independently of the others. There may be more than 200 suckers on an arm. Each one can feel, taste, and tightly grip whatever it touches.

Beak

Within an octopus's mouth is the one good-sized part of its body that is hard and inflexible: its beak. Its only other hard parts are a ribbon of tiny teeth, called the **radula**, near the mouth.

Just a few species of octopus—especially the giant Pacific octopus—grow large. Most are much smaller; many can nestle in the palm of your hand. Octopuses differ dramatically in other ways, too, as shown here.

The California lilliput octopus is Earth's smallest known octopus. Arms and all, it measures no more than an inch long. The Caribbean pygmy octopus is bigger, but its arms are less than four inches long. It often hides in empty snail and clam shells, or even in empty bottles on the seafloor.

The giant Pacific octopus hunts for food in both shallow and deep waters. It can travel a mile deep in search of prey. Each arm can measure more than six feet long. Males of this species can weigh a hundred pounds, and females about sixty pounds, but few grow to be that big with the average at about twenty-five pounds.

The mimic octopus lives in shallow waters near Indonesia. Like all octopuses, it can change its looks but does so in special ways. It can look *and* swim like a slender sea snake, a flat flounder, or a dangerous lionfish (which it mimics here).

The flapjack devilfish is sometimes called a jellyfish octopus. Its jelly-like body helps it survive the great water pressure in the deep where it lives. On its legs it has both suckers and thin fingers of skin, called cirri. They help the octopus hunt for food in total darkness by sense of touch, and by detecting chemicals in the water (like odors in the air).

Measuring Octopuses
In an instant, an octopus can change its mantle shape or make its arms short or long. Researchers do not rely on measurements of length; they consider octopus weight to be a more reliable measure, since that does not change.

An imaginary octopus attack

12

People used to fear octopuses. In the 1800s, fiction writers made up stories of octopuses attacking ships and divers. These imaginary monsters were sometimes called "devilfish." Later, octopuses were portrayed as dangerous animals in many movies. Real octopuses rarely harm people. Big or little, they avoid humans, either by hiding or fleeing. However, if an octopus is accidentally stepped on or grabbed, it may defend itself. It might bite with its beak, though this is uncommon.

All octopuses have poison that helps them subdue prey, but just four octopus species can be deadly to people. These four kinds of small blue-ringed octopuses live in the shallow sea waters of Australia and Indonesia. Among the most deadly animals on Earth, they bite with a nerve poison that can kill a human within minutes. Like all octopuses, they avoid people. Swimmers and divers are warned to watch out for them, and blue-ringed octopuses cause very few deaths.

No hard shells protect the soft bodies of octopuses. They are hunted by sharks, halibut, moray eels, barracudas, sea otters, seals, and many other sharp-toothed **predators**. How can they survive?

One way is to lose an arm, then escape. Nerves in the arm keep its muscles working for a few moments, and the still-wiggling arm is eaten by the predator while the octopus flees and hides. An octopus can survive very well with seven arms. Over many weeks, a new arm grows.

An octopus can also get away by releasing a cloud of dark ink through its funnel. If necessary, it can quickly squirt ink several times. The ink is stored in a sac within its mantle. It usually forms a big loose cloud, but some octopuses can squirt ink into a "decoy"—an octopus-shaped cloud. An ink cloud may contain chemicals that irritate a predator's eyes, or block its sense of smell. This can be vital. Moray eels, for example, hunt more by scent than by sight.

For a quick escape, an octopus can jet away. Its strong mantle muscles force out a quick burst of water. This pushes the octopus's body through the water—just as air rushing from a balloon can cause it to zoom across a room. To jet again, the octopus must take water into its mantle cavity, then squirt it out once more.

An octopus fleeing from danger can also try to find shelter. It can squeeze its body through a small opening—one that is too tiny for a predator. Here's an amazing fact! If an octopus's beak—its only inflexible part—can pass through an opening, its whole body can, too.

*Octopuses that live in the deep ocean, like the flapjack devilfish, do not produce ink. In their lightless world, ink would be useless. However, some deep-ocean octopuses may have "glow-in-the-dark" **bioluminescence** that lures prey animals close, or helps scare away predators.*

The most amazing of all octopus escape "tricks" is the ability to change the color and texture of their skin as well as their shape. In less than a second, an octopus can change to look like a sandy sea bottom, a bumpy rock, or part of a colorful coral reef. Of course, an octopus's camouflage can also help it hunt, by surprising a crab, fish, or other prey.

Within octopus skin are as many as two million tiny sacs called **chromatophores**. Each one contains a color—red, yellow, or brown. Muscles tighten or loosen the chromatophores to control what colors and amounts of colors are displayed. An octopus can also create patterns of spots or stripes. Beneath the chromatophores are cells that act like tiny mirrors. They reflect light. If an octopus is hiding in a place that is mostly green, these cells reflect that color. Also, octopus skin has muscles that can make its surface look smooth or bumpy.

Hunting predators often look for the eyes of the prey they're seeking. Octopuses can disguise their eyes with color patterns. They can also create bumps on the skin around their eyes. And they can produce lines on their skin that match up with the slit pupils of the eyes and help hide them. Predators also have a "search image" in their brains when they hunt, a picture of what they're looking for—just as a person does when looking for a misplaced cell phone, book, or other object. By continually changing their shape and colors, octopuses can mismatch a predator's "search image" and confuse it.

Lizards called chameleons are well-known for quickly changing their body colors. However, they are slowpokes compared to octopuses. An octopus's skin can look dramatically different in a small fraction of a second—and that is just the start of an octopus's camouflage ability. Given a little more time, the octopus also changes the shape of its mantle and arms so that it seems to disappear in its habitat.

Both humans and octopus predators can be fooled by an octopus's "moving rock" trick. Octopuses have been filmed crossing a dangerous open sandy area disguised as a rock covered with seaweed. The "rock" moves slowly. The "seaweed" sways as though it was pushed by currents. Then, when the "rock" reaches a coral reef or other hiding place, it disappears as the octopus blends into its new surroundings.

Can you find six octopuses hidden on these pages?
(Check your searching success on page 31.)

While avoiding predators, octopuses themselves catch and eat a lot of animals. They consume a great variety of sea life, including crabs, fish, and shrimp. They also eat many of their distant relatives—clams and all sorts of other shelled mollusks. They also eat close relatives: other octopuses!

Octopuses often hunt at night. They leave their dens and move through the water, sometimes fast, sometimes slow. They may jet for short distances. They usually crawl, or walk on the tips of their arms. Sometimes all eight arms hunt at once. They probe little hideouts for prey. They tip over rocks or coral pieces, then grab the crab or fish that was hiding there. With a blast of water from their funnels, they blow away sand to expose hidden crabs. Sometimes an octopus does a "web over." It settles down on the seafloor or an area of reef with the webs between its arms spread out. It covers an area like a blanket, then goes after the animals that are trapped beneath. When an octopus catches a crab, a chemical from the octopus's saliva starts digestion of its food even before it disappears down its mouth.

A web over

Clams and other mollusks with shells are easy to catch but not always easy to open. First, an octopus tries a quick, simple method: it uses its suckers and arms to pull apart the two halves of a clam's shell. If a mollusk's muscles are too strong, the octopus can use its beak to chip away part of the shell. Or it can drill a hole in the mollusk shell using its radula. When chipping or drilling creates a small opening, the octopus secretes a chemical into the mollusk. This chemical weakens the clam's muscles so the shell halves can be pulled apart easily.

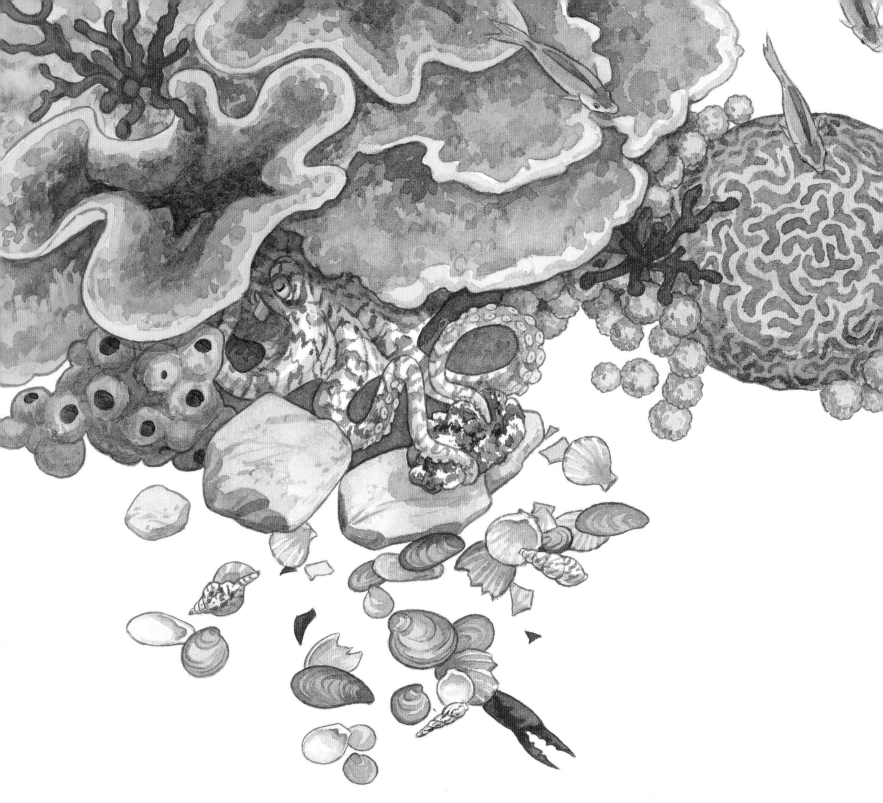

Octopuses often bring food home and eat in the safety of their dens. They toss out crab claws, clam shells, and other leftovers. Piles of these wastes are called **middens**. Scientists look for telltale middens when they search for octopus dens.

Octopus dens have small openings to help keep predators out. Often an octopus rearranges pieces of coral or other objects to make the den entrance even smaller. All sorts of places can hide octopuses, even trash discarded by humans. For example, when a scientist looked in nine beer bottles on the bottom of Washington's Puget Sound, each one was the den of a small red octopus.

Octopuses change dens as they grow in size, or when food gets scarce in the neighborhood. But they always keep their dens neat and clean. They do daily housekeeping, blowing out sand, gravel, and bits of uneaten food with bursts of water from their funnels.

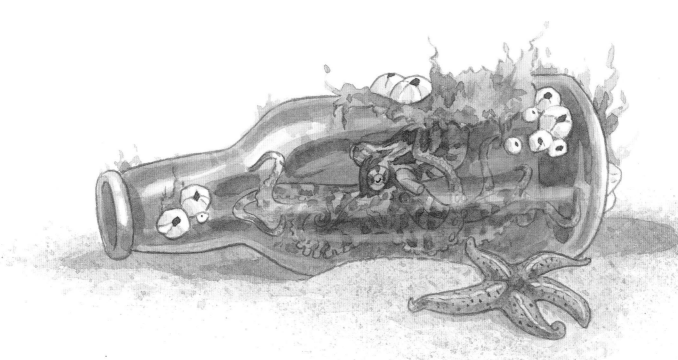

An octopus never shares its den with another octopus. They are always alone, except briefly at mating time. Octopuses mate near the end of their lives. A male or female octopus may find its mate by sight, or by visiting dens. Scientists believe that female octopuses may also release a scent in the water that attracts males.

After mating, females of some octopus species continue to live out in the open. Blue-ringed octopuses do this, with eggs attached under the webs that stretch between their arms. However, most species lay their eggs within a den. Some species hang many thousands of eggs, each about the size of a grain of rice, in dangling clusters. Others glue about a hundred larger eggs to the den's walls or ceiling.

Often a female octopus moves stones to completely block her den's opening. Now her home is much more than a hideout. It is a nursery for a whole new generation.

Eggs

"Super Mom" seems like a good name for a female octopus. She guards her eggs from being eaten. She keeps them clean, wiping them with suckers on the tips of her arms and squirting them with water from her funnel. This also brings oxygen to the young as they develop within the eggs.

Week after week, an octopus mother is steadfast. The time needed for the eggs to hatch varies with the octopus species and with water temperature. In warm tropical waters, the eggs can hatch in a few weeks. In the colder north, a giant Pacific octopus mother may stand guard for as long as six months.

During the entire time, an octopus mom usually doesn't leave her den. She doesn't eat, and loses half of her weight. Her skin turns pale. When her young hatch, she may help them out of the den. She widens the opening and pushes them out with bursts of water. Then she dies. By this time, the father of the young is also dead. After mating, males stop hiding in dens and stop eating. They are easy prey for predators, or starve to death.

Hatchling from large egg

Hatchling from small egg

The tiny hatchlings from the smallest eggs have stubby arms. At first, their ability to produce ink and change color is not well developed. They swim and drift in ocean currents as they grow. Many are snared by jellyfish, or gulped down by fish or other predators. Only a few out of every thousand live very long.

Larger hatchlings from bigger eggs have long arms. These hatchlings, often from deep-sea species, are able to change color, spew out ink, jet, and hide. Right after hatching they try to survive on the seafloor. Fish, crabs, and eels catch some, but more of these bigger hatchlings escape.

Big or little, most young octopuses die, but the survivors grow fast. They may live long enough to mate, and produce a new octopus generation.

Each year many thousands of tons of octopuses are caught for people to eat, especially in Europe and Asia. However, some people choose not to eat octopuses because they admire these creatures so much.

In the wild and in captivity, octopuses show feelings or moods by changing color. They turn pale with fear. They flash red when annoyed or angry. Captive octopuses can be shy or aggressive, but also friendly or playful. They often have favorite foods, and favorite people. Sometimes an octopus dislikes one person in a laboratory or aquarium. When that person comes close, the octopus might squirt him or her with a jet of water.

Captive octopuses are given chances to show their intelligence. They solve mazes and can learn to do a task by watching another octopus do it. They can get at food that is inside a glass jar, closed with a cork or with a screw cap lid. Using their suckers, they pull out the cork, or turn the lid counterclockwise to get the treat.

Scientists are still full of questions about octopuses. Little is known about many species, especially those of the deep ocean. Even close-to-shore species still hold many mysteries. For example, how do octopuses, which do not see color, "know" in their brain how to camouflage themselves so well? We can all look forward to discovering more about some of the smartest animals in the sea.

Glossary

bioluminescence—Light given off by living organisms, including fireflies, fungi, bacteria, and some deep-ocean fishes and octopuses.

cartilage—A tough, flexible material that forms the supportive pen within squid bodies.

cephalopods—Ocean-living mollusks that have arms or tentacles attached to their heads.

chromatophores—Tiny color-filled sacks in octopus skin. An octopus can enlarge or reduce the size of chromatophores in order to show different colors and patterns on its skin.

funnel—A tube that can squirt water, ink, and wastes out of the body of a cephalopod. (Also called a siphon.)

gills—An organ in fishes, octopuses, and many other water-dwelling animals that removes vital oxygen from water.

invertebrate—Animals without backbones, including mollusks, crustaceans, insects, and spiders.

mantle—The large baglike sac above, or behind, an octopus's head that holds its gills, hearts, stomach, and other organs.

middens—Piles of shells and other remains of prey that octopuses discard at the entrances to their dens.

mollusks—Soft-bodied animals without backbones, most of which have a protective shell. They include snails, clams, chambered nautiluses, and octopuses.

octopodes—The plural of the word "octopus." Saying either "octopuses" or "octopodes" is correct. "Octopi" is not, because the original name of octopus came from Greek, not Latin.

predators—Animals that catch and eat other animals.

radula—The hard-edged ribbon of teeth that an octopus can use to drill into a mollusk shell, in order to help it get to the soft-bodied mollusk within.

tentacles—Long, flexible limbs of squids, nautiluses, and cuttlefish. Octopuses have no tentacles.

To Learn More

Books and Periodicals

Blaxland, Beth. *Octopuses, Squids, and Their Relatives*. Philadelphia, PA: Chelsea House, 2003.

Cerullo, Mary. *The Octopus: Phantom of the Sea*. NY: Dutton, 1997.

Jango-Cohen, Judith. *Octopuses*. Tarrytown, NY: Benchmark, 2004.

Mather, Jennifer. "*Eight Arms, With Attitude*." Natural History, Feb. 2007, pp. 30–36.

Trueit, Trudi Strain. *Octopuses, Squids, and Cuttlefish*. NY: Franklin Watts, 2002.

Websites*

aqua.org The National Aquarium in Baltimore has information about the giant Pacific octopus, with photos and video.

marine.alaskapacific.edu Information about the giant Pacific octopus

montereybayaquarium.org Click on "Animals and Experiences," then on several octopus species.

sciencefriday.com Click on "watch," then under "popular videos," click on "Where's the Octopus?"

thecephalopodpage.org

Answer key for pages 18–19

*Websites active at time of publication.

Index